Kunolúkhwa Means I Love You:
Oneida Stories from an Elder Grandmother and Her Grandson

By Eleanor Bailey & Dr. Thomas James Reed, PhD

Cover by Norma Skenandore Primeau

ISBN: 978-1-953216-00-7

© 2023 Dr. Thomas James Reed, PhD

INTRODUCTION

My grandma and I are on a journey to preserve the library inside her head and heart before it burns down. We, as Haudenosaunee, as Oneida people, are our stories. Stories are our portal to the past and a portal into the roots of our family tree. If I let my grandmother talk, the stories pour out. Her story is my story. Her blood runs through me. Through a compilation of short stories, memories, and conversations, we strive to offer wisdom and insight as an Oneida Tribal elder and her grandson based on the history of our family, community, Tribe, and culture.

Everything we do is to honor our ancestors and pave the way for seven generations to come. We reach back generations to understand where we are now and where we are headed. Yawʌ?kó, thank you in Oneida.

ACKNOWLEDGMENTS

Yawʌʔkó, Great Creator. As is said in the California State University of Long Beach, known as Cal State Puvungna's student song, *"Students, the people are anxious and excited to see what you will do with your education. Go forth and work hard for them."*

To all the relatives behind us and in front of us.

TABLE OF CONTENTS

Preface

    I.   Kahwá·tsíleʔ: Family

Go Pack Go
She Has Good Words
He is a Good Man
The People That Built Me
Generations
Realizing
Why Not
Take Care
Casinos
"Auntie" Dill
Anderson Cornelius
Exiles
Blood Memories
He Never Came Home
Strangers
Perspective
Haskell
Cousin Angel
Cornelius
Ohana

    II.   Acknowledge, Educate, and Honor

Traditional Names
Pow Wow
Community Peacemaking
Value
Oneida Hymn Singers
Family Gathering
Christianity and Colonization
Constitution
The Other Side
Hierarchy
I Understand
Assassin's Creed 3
Thanksgiving & Native American Heritage Day
Santa's Real
Hoyá·nl Happy New Year
Reservation Dogs
Civilization

Drum
Intergenerational Trauma and Intergenerational Resiliency
Garden
Homecoming
Pendleton

    III.   Good Man and Good Words

License
Truth
Keys
Remembering
Drawing the Circle Bigger
First Dream
5/25/21
Love Cups
Great Grandkids
Grace
Smile
Everything
Proud
Time
Happy to Get to Know Anyone
Technology
Beaded Eagle Feather
Respect and Sharing
Bragging
Someday
Never Alone
First
Always Remember
NʌkiʔwaH, Until Next Time

Appendix

PREFACE

Grandma's Roller Skates

I wanted to roller skate
Older kids would go into Green Bay to skate
I could never go
My parents would get cases of canned milk we would drink
Half and half with water
Bought it by the case
If you saved so many wrappers you could get different prizes
I got roller skates that clipped on
Clipped onto your shoes
My mom and dad
We had nothing but dust and dirt around the house
They put cement for a 10 feet long sidewalk
To get the water from the pump to the house
I would skate on it

Dolls

Me and my cousins
Made 'em out of slats
I don't know where we got these slats
My parents, they never took anything away from us
Whatever we found we could play with
We got a nail and a hammer
You could make them as tall as you wanted to
We made them almost as tall as us
You'd put a slat for arms
Drew a face on it
Used binder twine from all the farmers around
And nailed it on top for their hair

I. Kahwá·tsíleʔ: Family

Go Pack Go

This story starts from the hazy, smokers section outside of Chicago O'Hare International Airport to my final destination of Green Bay, WI. Go Pack, Go. I was born in Tacoma, Washington in 1989 to my loving parents Michelle Bailey Reed and Steve "Twiggs" Martin Reed. I have two older sisters, Katelyn Michelle Reed, married name Valentine and my oldest sister, Chelsea Marie Reed, married name Sterrett. As I travel, I leave my beautiful wife, Julia, and two cute white puppies, Sydney and Millie, waiting for me at home in California.

The story I am telling, during this time in our existence and consciousness, is a dual perspective: telling my story and relaying my grandma's story as best I can.

I have visited my grandmother a number of times on the Oneida Nation, or the Oneida Reservation, right outside of Green Bay, Wisconsin. I have not visited my grandma in Wisconsin for 4 years, since 2017. I will be savoring every minute soaking up Granny's energy.

I had last visited Oneida to help film a lacrosse documentary that January, then returned in July to host a screening of a lacrosse film, *Spirit Game: Pride of a Nation*. My grandmother, cousin Norma, and Great Aunt Josie, all supported me during the film screening sitting behind me in the front rows in the Oneida Business Committee Chambers.

This visit feels particularly special. I feel a calling to document Granny's stories, the library inside her head and heart. If I let her talk, the stories pour out. We are our stories.

Stories are our portal to the past, a portal into the roots of our family tree. Together, we are to document them before they get lost amid the sands of time.

There is so much to say, yet so little time.
 As author of the "MAUS" graphic novels, Art Spiegelman says, "My family bleeds history."

I trust the Creator will guide our conversation how it is needed.

Here we go, into the past. Wish us luck.

She Has Good Words

Ever since I was 13, 19 years ago, my parents have told me to cherish my time with my grandma, as every time I see her could be the last time. So I did. And I plan to.

We call her Granny Bird. I do not know why, but we have since I was a kid.

Granny is full Oneida and an elder in our Tribe. She is the knowledge carrier, the wise one. Her Ukwehu·wé (Oneida) name is, "She has Good Words." She is a living saint in my eyes.

She always told me she had a special place in her heart for me. I have a special place in my heart for her. A part of me feels home when I am with her in Oneida. I am who I am because of who she is. I draw my strength from her.

My grandma is how I can connect with the Creator, by seeing her model how to have a seamless fusion of our old, traditional beliefs as Ukwehu·wé (the Oneida word for Original People) with a western, Christian perspective.

An Indigenous graphic novel collection, "Moonshot," said, "My grandmothers and my aunties are my superheroes." My parents, God bless em', were loving and hardworking, and whenever they could not be there to pick us up from school because of work, superhero Granny Bird was there to save the day. She was always there to save the day.

My grandmother is very patriotic and very Christian. She is devout, caring, sweet, filled with endless hope, and steadfast in the American Dream. Only once in my life have I seen my grandmother without hope, and that was right after her best friend and brother passed away, Harrison Cornelius. Feeling hopeless, she scolded me for being too nice to a waitress because she said people would think I was being disingenuous. This happened one time. All the rest of the time, she makes me look like a grumpy grinch when I am on my best behavior. People who know me would tell you I am annoyingly optimistic and kind, so that is saying something.

Granny attended a classroom with all grade levels up to 8th grade in one single room. She then went to Freedom High School. She is brilliant, one of the smartest people I know, proving that a piece of paper does not measure a person's intelligence and intelligence is not defined by a degree.

My grandma was one of 12, the eldest female of the remaining of her 6 siblings.

Here are some words from her, *"My family is everything. Probably because I grew up in a big family and always knew I had someone I knew I could depend on with 9 brothers and sisters."*

She had 2 kids, and many of her siblings had kids, and they had kids, and so on. I lost count 7 years ago after I had gotten to 115 or 120 and counting of my relatives in Oneida, Wisconsin. With every Oneida visit, I meet more relatives I am related to, whether at an Oneida Business Committee meeting, the gas station, Walmart, or The Golden Basket diner. Now I am surprised if I do not meet someone new I am related to.

He is a Good Man

Wakenyâhtâ niwakiʔtaló·tâ, I am Turtle Clan. Ukwehu·wé níʔi, I am Oneida. Onâyoteʔa·ká niʔi, I am People of the Standing Stone. Lukwe'tiyó ní yúkyats, He is a Good Man is my name in Oneida. My English name is Dr. Thomas James Reed.

I am inspired by the way people in Oneida see the spirit world. The spirit world is more real to me than the physical world, and it has been since I was about 5 years old. I love the spirit, the Great Creator, and I love how people in Oneida play the Spirit Game, the Creator's Game, the Medicine Game, they-bump-hips, also known as lacrosse.

I have a PhD in Leadership Studies from the University of San Diego and did my dissertation on Oneida college lacrosse players' perspectives of the sacred game of lacrosse using talking circles. I have a Master's in Public Administration and a Certificate in American Indian Studies from California State University, Long Beach and a Bachelor's in Communication with an emphasis in Rhetoric and Leadership from Pepperdine University. I am a Restorative Practices consultant and practitioner. I am a tenure track professor in American Indian Studies at California State University of Long Beach and I teach Restorative Justice in Indigenous Communities at Vermont Law School. I am a lacrosse commentator and have been playing lacrosse since 1999. I am the program manager for the Haudenosaunee Nationals Development Teams. My heart bleeds for public service and I hope to hold political office. My mission is leaving this world a better place for seven generations to come.

With that said, I was a terrible student in elementary school, middle school, high school, and for the first 2 years of my undergraduate. I was extremely passive with my education and would put in just enough effort to scrape by.

I tell my students now as an Assistant Professor, you get what you put into it, and I was not putting much into *my academic education growing up.*

One summer, while visiting Oneida, I took an online accounting course and I was essentially attempting to teach myself accounting from square one. I got a B on a test, after studying for hours. I told my grandma and asked if she was proud of me, and she would sigh and say, *"Well, I just know if you put your mind to it, you could get an A. You could excel if you just try a little harder."*

And I would say, "Grandma, that's mean."
She would respond, *"What? It's true."*

My grandma would always tell me she knows how smart and brilliant I could be if I just applied myself. This would make me more upset and would make me want to try less for some reason. It takes time for me to learn certain lessons, which I am still learning as I write. My grandma has taught me a lot.

The truth was, I could do better. She knew I was capable of more when I thought I was simply not a good student. My grandma's belief in me changed my view of myself as a scholar, a student, a lifelong learner.

After dropping out of college twice and into my junior year, it hit me that I must take charge of my education. I finished my undergraduate, then went on to receive my masters and doctorate.

She tells me, *"I wouldn't have pushed you if I didn't think you could do it."*

She was right.
And for that, I say, yawʌʔkó, thank you in Oneida, grandma.

The People That Built Me

Yawʌ?kó, thank you, family, I am who I am, because of you.

I came from two very loving parents who met and fell in love young. I have had the privilege to watch their love mature as they have. Words of affirmation and hugs are abundant in their home. As a family growing up and to this day, we express our love and care for one another generously.

My mom, Michelle Bailey Reed, has the biggest, beautiful heart. Her laugh is contagious, her prayers are abundant, and her personality is loveable. Everyone is a friend to my mom. She lives her life others-focused and spends her time deeply loving and caring for others. As a natural hostess, she makes everyone who steps foot into their home feel as if she is their mother or best friend. My mom has served others as a dental hygienist for over 3 decades and taught my sisters and I a strong work ethic. Outside of work, my mom spends her time mentoring and loving on younger generations. I have learned from my mom how to love well, include everyone, create harmony, be a light, walk with joy, spread kindness, and feel deeply for others with my whole being. I love you so much, Mom. I am so grateful for the love you so freely give and everything you have done to allow me to live the life I do now.

My dad is my best friend. I call my dad, Twiggs Reed, Coach, because he was my high school cross country coach. I have countless memories of my dad's words echoing in my head during some of my most physically challenging moments while running. I was able to drown out everyone else's voice and hear his. He is a servant leader and one of the best orators I have ever witnessed. He is a man of integrity, character, honesty, and faithfulness. He looks people in the eye, gives a strong handshake, and truly sees them for their heart. He walks alongside others to mentor them and pour into them. I have learned from my dad that the most important thing is to be able to look myself in the mirror and know that I am a man of integrity. He always taught me actions speak louder than words.

He passed on to me my English and Irish heritage, and has always supported my passion for my Oneida culture. He attended his first Pow Pow around 2011. He talked about witnessing the dancers and hearing the powerful drummers and singers. He told me, "I get why you do what you do." His unwavering love and support for me is a gift from God I will forever cherish.

My eldest sister, Chelsea Marie Sterrett, and her husband, Nick, are intelligent, brilliant, caring, and kind. Family means everything to Chelsea, and I have had the privilege to witness her pour her heart and soul into raising her two daughters, Hazel Katerina and Penelope Rey, and son, Archer Cornelius. They have given their children childhood memories full of love, learning, and adventure. As a teacher, my sister shares not only her knowledge, but gives her heart to her students. She helps them learn academically and grow personally because of her love and care. As the oldest sibling, Chelsea has always been a leader, paving the way for my sister, Katelyn, and I through life. She sees the world through the lens of a distinguished scientist and researcher, thinking critically and intrigued by the world around her in all its wonder. She teaches me something every day as we learn alongside each other through life.

My second oldest sister, Katelyn Michelle Valentine, is a person I aspire to be like. She is compassionate, kind, and empathetic. She values inclusivity and equality. Katelyn is thoughtful in her words and conscientious in her actions. She loves the underdog, welcomes the outcasts, and remembers those forgotten. Her ability to be authentic to herself invites others to do the same. She reminds me that I can come home to myself. Katelyn has taught me to question everything and that truth has no fear from investigation. At life's great crossroads, I have come to Katelyn shattered in pieces. She welcomes me with open arms, helping pick up the pieces with care, fun, laughter, and reassurance. Her husband, Chris Valentine, loves my sister wholeheartedly. I appreciate his caring heart, sincerity, and authenticity.

Aknulha nukwa – My mother's side

I admire my Uncle Mike, my grandma's favorite son as she calls him and my mom's brother. He thinks outside of the box, walks to the beat of his own drum, and speaks from the heart. I enjoy his refreshing outlook on life whenever we converse and he encourages me to challenge the status quo.

My cousin Norma Skenandore Primeau is one of the kindest human beings I know. She has one of the biggest and most beautiful hearts this world has seen. Norma's Oneida name reflects this as it translates to, "She is Friendly." I trust, love, and adore the incredible person she is. She is a gifted beader and has beaded my Oneida regalia and graduation regalia to help me represent my Oneida heritage to the world. I love her husband, my cousin Frank, as we have many fond memories together.

My Great Aunt Josie, whose Oneida name means, "The Eagles are Dancing," is full of life. Alongside her husband, my Great Uncle Tom, life is always an adventure.

I am grateful my Oneida family tree spreads far and wide. I am thankful for my grandma's parents, my great grandparents, Anderson William Cornelius and Liliane Wheelock Cornelius, and their children, in order from eldest to youngest: my late Great Aunt Ella May and late Great Uncle Mike; my late Great Aunt Delores and my late Great Uncle Zack; my late Great Uncle Harry and my late Great Aunt Diane; my late Great Uncle Lincoln who passed at age 26 and was never married; my Great Uncle Frank and Great Aunt Nancy; my Great Uncle Leonard and Great Aunt Yvonne; my Great Uncle Clarence and Great Aunt Sandy; my dear grandmother, Eleanor Bailey; the late Melvin and late Liliane Pauline, two babies who died in infancy; my late Great Uncle Ben and Great Aunt Jerry; and my Great Aunt Josie and Great Uncle Tom. This gratitude continues for my grandma's siblings' children, and their children's children, and all the family spanning across Turtle Island.

My love, my wife, Julia Elizabeth Reed

I have never cared for anyone in this universe like I do for my Jewel. Tears flow from my eyes when I think of the gift, honor, and privilege it is to be the luckiest person in the world to be with her. The easiest and best decision I have ever made was to marry Julia. When I first met Julia, I had a renewed sense of hope in the world knowing she existed. She is kind, positive, spirit-filled, and loving. I would drive to the moon and back just to see Julia's eyes for a moment. Her smile lights my spirit on fire. I love you, Jewel. You are the other part of my soul. Chief Oren Lyons, Faithkeeper of the Onondaga, was once speaking with Julia and me. He turned to her and said, "You are his strength." I know this to be true.

Generations

My loving mom, Michelle Marie Reed, articulated her reflections,

"When I was growing up in the 60's to 70's, it was about assimilation into society. My mom didn't teach my brother or I much about what it is to be Native. Our German-Irish dad was so proud of my mom and her heritage. Most of what I learned growing up came from my dad.

However, after we were out of the home, my mom reclaimed her Native identity and leaned more fully into it with the chance to make sure nothing more was lost with her grandchildren. She shared and taught you and your sisters wonderful parts that had laid dormant in her heart.

Those early years in Bellevue, Washington while you were growing up in private school, gave you precious times with your grandma for a few hours a couple times a week while I worked as a dental hygienist. Grandma lived close enough for sleepovers with you and your sisters, creating a chance to learn about our Oneida family and stories from her youth."

Growing up, my mom witnessed discrimination against Native peoples. Hearing my own sweet mother discuss the assimilation she lived transports me back to my learnings as a student. Her story is echoed across Indian Country, in the wake of the Indian Boarding Schools, forced assimilation, and genocide. I am able to see firsthand how colonization is relevant and woven into my own family's history. I am grateful to my mother who has welcomed my learnings with open arms and an open heart, and we can learn side by side about the ancestors who paved the way for us. My grandmother and mother have shattered the chain of intergenerational trauma with intergenerational love.

My grandmother is the matrilineal leader for our family. She passed down my families' clan of the Turtle Clan to my mother who passed it down to my sisters and I. This is a gift and an honor I do not have the ability to do because we as Oneida, are a matrilineal society, however, my sisters are able to pass on the Turtle clan identity to their children.

Professor Georgiana Sanchez, a Chumash and Tohono O'Ohdam elder, voiced during an American Indian Literature course I took with her in the spring of 2014 that sometimes the desire to learn about heritage can skip a generation due to assimilation and colonization. This cultural unlearning is not their fault, but a direct consequence of the indoctrination. In the words of Dr. Antonio Jiménez-Luque, a member of my PhD dissertation committee in 2020 vocalized, "Colonization exists in the minds of the oppressed and the oppressor."

In my 2018 leadership theory class, Professor Afsaneh Nahavandi, who was born in Iran, told the class how often the first generation of immigrants to a country maintain their previous cultures, often the second generation of immigrants can have a desire to assimilate and leave behind the previous generations' culture, and oftentimes it is the third generation of immigrants who once again revive and reclaim their families' cultural heritage and traditions. This provides clarity on the nuances of how cultural identity can skip generations.

Despite the assimilation my family experienced and the deleterious effects of colonization, Native Americans were making progress in the American Indian Movement (AIM), an organization at work still to this day. The Occupation of Alcatraz was happening in 1969 to 1971, which was a 19-month occupation by Native American students and activists who formed a group called, "the Indians of All Tribes" as well as members of AIM. They were acting on the Fort Laramie Treaty of 1868, which stated any federal lands no longer being used could be used for Native Tribes, in an effort to draw attention to the broken treaties and oppression of Native peoples by the Federal government. The Trail of Broken Treaties occurred in 1972, where a caravan of activists traveled from the West Coast to DC with a 21-point proposal of demands and ended in an eight day occupation of the Department of the Interior, where the Bureau of Indian Affairs is located. The Red Power Movement occurred in the 1960s to 1970s within the human rights movement as a social movement which demanded self-determination for Native peoples. This progress came from grassroots efforts of Indigenous organizers who fought for their ancestors and their descendants. In doing so, one day, may we all acknowledge, educate, and honor Indigenous peoples. May we be free to embody the fullness of our Native identity. May we seek justice for oppression faced and make right the inequities occurring against our peoples.

Realizing

My grandma asked me, *"How old were you when you realized I was Native American? What caused you to pursue this interest?"*

One of my first memories as a child was exploring my grandma's house in Renton, Washington. I remember seeing moccasins and noticing cradleboards hung on the wall. I remember seeing pictures in Granny's photo album of me in the cradleboard from when I was a newborn. I remember Native American paintings decorating her walls. She had Native American character salt and pepper shakers and Native American dolls. Her house was infused with Native American cultural artifacts that I recall from my earliest childhood memories.

The curiosity I remember from appreciating these artifacts was the first glimpse I had of wanting to uncover more about our families' Native American heritage.

My grandma's authentic cultural expression sparked the journey that has inspired me to connect with my Native ancestors and help educate, honor, and acknowledge Indigenous culture and ways to the world.

Why Not

"Grandma, why did you move out of Oneida, Wisconsin to the Pacific Northwest in the first place?"

"I was working for the telephone company doing blueprinting for the engineering department in Milwaukee, Wisconsin, the town next to Oneida. It was one of my first big jobs. My sister's youngest son, Timmy, was only four years old. He was a very healthy boy until he was about 3 years old. Then, he started to say his head was hurting him. They started taking him to different doctors to see what was wrong.

They took him to nine different doctors, and the doctors would say, 'There is nothing wrong with him, he is a healthy little boy. He just hears you talking about it. He is healthy. There is nothing wrong with him.'

Finally, they went to a neurologist who specializes in the brain. Timmy was diagnosed with brain cancer. After meeting with the neurosurgeon, there was a 50/50 chance the doctor would be able to remove the cancer.

His parents decided to go ahead with the operation. If there was any chance at all, they were going to try. Once the surgeon started operating, he found the cancer had grown too far.

There was nothing they could do.

They brought him home from the hospital. He had to have 24-hour care. I quit my job and moved back home [to Oneida, Wisconsin] *to take care of him. I was just a teenager and used to pretend he was my baby because I loved him so much.*

He only lasted about a month. He was in so much pain. He could not open his eyes, hardly at all. So Delores asked him, 'Timmy, do you want to go to be with Jesus now?' He shook his head yes.

She released him and he died the next day.

My brother and his wife came home for the funeral. They were stationed in Nevada. They asked me, "You don't have a job and you don't owe any bills, why don't you come back with us and you can get a job with the government?"

I didn't even consider it at first. They were on a 30-day leave. The day before they left, I thought, 'Well, why not.' I told them I would go with them. I threw a piece of luggage together and went back with them.

I took the civil service exams. I had passed them all.

But there were no jobs open at the time. I thought, 'As long as I'm out West, I'll go up to Seattle to visit my sister more. I'll stay with her and get a job out there for a little while.'

She left home when I was too young and I didn't really know her. I thought I would go stay with her, get to know her, and work out there for a while.

I was working when I met Chuck Bailey. We got married and I stayed in Seattle."

Take Care

I love understanding my grandma more. I love learning everything she has gone through for our family and what has led her to where she is now.

Her story is my story. Her blood runs through me.

"What made you want to go back to Oneida in 2008 after living in Seattle?"

"I was working at JCPenney. Most of my family had gotten a job and moved away from home. People were all living in Tennessee, California, and Washington.

Our family was really close and had always depended on each other. We were there for one another.

When I retired from JCPenney, my brothers asked me when I was going to move back home. When they had retired, they moved home.

I decided to move back to Wisconsin to take care of my eldest sister, Delores. Auntie Dill. Norma, Delores' daughter, had been taking care of her. Delores had heart problems and diabetes. She had been on dialysis for years and needed someone there because she was really weak. Norma would take off from work to be with her mom. I moved back to Oneida to help take care of her. I found a house between my two sisters' houses and was near my family.

Delores died shortly after I moved back.

When I moved home, everything was so different. Buildings were gone and other businesses were put up."

"I love your heart. You are such a loving, incredible person. You returned to your roots."

"I felt like I always wanted to take care of my family anyway I could."

"You have taken care of your family and you still do. You take care of me all the time. You are so generous and loving."

"Yes. Well, you know I am just proud of you, and I love you so much."

"I am so proud of you, and I love you. You inspire me, motivate me, and teach me so much."

Casinos

We are on Granny's ottoman, which is fashioned to look like a little turtle, huddled together with my grandmother and her dog Elvis, a cute little Papillion.

She reads stories about her brother, Harrison.

My great Uncle Harry Anderson is named after my great grandfather and Harry's dad, Anderson William Cornelius. Harry was a character. A spirit full of energy. A laughter in the face of sickness. A smile in the face of pain.

I first met my Great Uncle Harrison when I was 19 and he was full of jokes. His cane had printed images of bingo, slot machines, and playing cards, and he would talk about his fun adventures.

Harry told me a story about going to casinos. He would tell me the different casino hotels would compensate people who gambled by providing them with free rooms, to encourage people to lose money at the casinos. My Great Uncle Harry would call ahead to set up a room, take out money from the hotel to insinuate he would be gambling there. Then instead of gambling, he would pocket the money and enjoy the free stay.

He loved that story. I had probably heard it three or so times.

My grandma is reading. She screens the pages intently looking for stories she wants to share. I imagine all the stories are worth sharing.

She passes me a story on a photocopied document.

Elvis, my grandma's Papillon, shoots up as the *WHOOP* of the pages hits the ground.

"Auntie" Dill

My grandma passed me documents of transcribed interviews from our relatives. I read about my Great Auntie Delores. Granny called her Dill. She was my grandmother's second oldest sister who passed away in 2007 before I got a chance to meet her.

Great Auntie Dill worked at a daycare as a bus driver. Her real nephews and nieces went to the daycare so they always called her Auntie Dill. After that, all the other kids called her Auntie, too. She said many children used to come up to her and call her Auntie in public places.

Anderson Cornelius

Great Auntie Dill spoke of my Great Grandfather, Anderson Cornelius, working in migrant type camps, which were separated by three cabins, "Mexicans, Jamaicans, and Oneidas." The notion of "divide and conquer" utilized by settler-colonists comes to mind.

I learned my great grandfather also worked in the cranberry marshes. My grandma loves this part of my great grandpa's life because she says it shows my great grandfather's character, integrity, and work ethic.

"He took any job available to support his many children, including working in the cranberry marshes when he had arthritis," my grandma shares.

Even though the marsh water was cold and flared my great grandfather Anderson's arthritis, he continued to show up and work hard for his family. My grandma tells me my great grandpa worked in the cranberry marshes *"until he became completely disabled and couldn't walk without crutches or a cane. He was in extreme pain for years with rheumatoid arthritis."* He worked until he was physically no longer able to.

My great grandfather's story embodies the many stories I hear and read from Oneida people: having a generous sense of humor, harboring love for your family and community, and igniting one another's flames through our own flame.

Great Auntie Dill says Great Grandpa Anderson was running around the train tracks when he fell. His friend, Chauncy Skenandore, thought Anderson had gotten run over by the train, and ran to him, but to his surprise, found Anderson laughing in the space between the ground and the tracks, as the train passed over him.

Great Auntie Dill described, "the basement of our log home always smelled good." I can practically smell the scents she describes, of apples, potatoes, carrots, beets, white and kidney beans, and wooden barrels of pickles and sauerkraut, which my great grandpa made. He would put a piece of wood with a stone on top to keep it weighted down, so the pickles would stay under the brine of water, vinegar, and his other flavorings. In Oneida, I have seen the outside of the log houses, some of which my Great Grandpa built, and I can envision Dill's description of the dirt floor of the basement ground with walls made of fieldstone.

Exiles

Dill says when they were kids, three little neighbor redhead kids would get mad at Dill, Eleanor (my grandma), and the rest of my family, and would say, "go back to where *you* came from."

My heart is heavy.

Chief Oren Lyons notions that the Haudenosaunee (Iroquois) and Indigenous people in general were exiled in the land of the free.

Where do the Indigenous peoples go in the land of the free, home of the brave, which was stolen from Indigenous peoples?

Dill talked about having to switch schools from Green Bay to De Pere because of the prejudice, discrimination, and racism she faced in Green Bay. While Green Bay is not far from De Pere, De Pere was closer to the Oneida Nation so they would likely have had more exposure to Oneida peoples.

Blood Memories

Sitting with my grandmother, I learned about how my Great Grandpa Anderson Cornelius had earned a certificate in bricklaying in Indian Boarding School.

My blood memories flooded back when my great grandpa said, "Of course it [Indian Boarding School] was hard, they were punished for speaking Oneida and many children ran away."

That stopped me in my tracks.

Wow. Something I already knew and teach about often, but it hits harder coming from the mouths of my relatives who lived it.

He Never Came Home

My Great Auntie Dill talked about having an Uncle Joshua that never returned from boarding school. My grandma recalls, *"We heard different stories, we just don't know what the truth is. No one really knew for sure."* I am filled with sadness and anger as I read Dill's words, frustrated at what my great, great uncle Joshua had to endure and frustrated I never knew.

When I see the numbers of all the children's bodies in graves at Indian Boarding/Residential Schools, I say to people, "These are children who never returned home, families without answers."

I guess I am one of those family members without answers about a relative who never returned from boarding school.

"I don't know what ever happened to him," my grandma says. *"We just knew he never came home,"* she tells me. I stare at my grandma as she stares at me. I wonder if I said something wrong. But she tells me she was just thinking about the truth of what happened to Joshua.

My grandmother gave me a pile of documents to read from Dill. As I relay some of the stories to my grandma, it makes her want to go back and reread her sister Dill's recollections.

Joshua's story lives on through us.

Strangers

My grandma says, *"Harry never met a stranger."*

She is telling me a story about eating at Iver's.
"Harry is talking with a couple about driving places and different trucks.
He said it like he knew them really well, like he had been driving with one of them for years.
The couple eventually gets up and leaves."

My grandma asks, *"Who was that?"*
My great Uncle Harrison replied, "I don't know."

I tell my grandma I try to live like Great Uncle Harry. I try to see everyone as a friend I just have yet to meet. His spirit continues.

Perspective

"When dad couldn't work anymore [because of his rheumatoid arthritis], *Harry as the oldest son, took responsibility and quit high school I believe his junior or senior year, to get a job at a lumber yard to support the family."*

"Harry got his own car when he was 17 from working with the farmers. That was hard work with the farmers. Harry would have to be up early in the morning to go to the farmer's place. Or bailing hay all day long. Harry used to always say about how strong his brother Lincoln was."

My grandma told me a story about Harry and Lincoln working, and I remember this story from when Harry would tell me: *"A big truck going through a field. People would have to pick up bales of hay on both sides and put them in the truck. Harry and another man working on one side, barely able to keep up. Lincoln would be doing it by himself on the other side, teasing them, and saying, 'You want me to come help you out over there?'"*

I had heard that story many times from Uncle Harry. Hearing it this time from my grandma's perspective, I still hear something new, like my Great Uncle Lincoln teasing my Great Uncle Harry. My grandma and her siblings, the Cornelius siblings, love to tease one another.

"Harry and Lincoln later joined the Army so they could send Mom money."

Haskell

My grandma wanted to go to Haskell Indian School, a Tribal College, located in Lawrence, Kansas.

My grandma said, *"I don't know if it was a college or trade school. I always wanted to be a nurse because I always wanted to help people. That was what I was going to go to school for."*

She did not get acceptance until too late. She received word through a telegram stating, "You are authorized to report to Haskell immediately." It arrived the day before class.

"I thought, well, too late now." My grandma says, *"I went to work instead."*

"They accepted me too late. I had other plans by then. When I thought I was going to go to Haskell, I saved up money. I never got a reply from them, so I quit saving my money. When I was notified at the last second, I decided not to go."

"Your dream lives on inside of me. When I go to Harvard next week, you will be going to Harvard with me."

"Oh, yes, yes. That is so exciting."

A lot of friends and people grandma knew went to Haskell.
My Great Uncle Leonard went to Haskell Indian School.

"All Nations went there," my grandma tells me. *"Sioux, BlackFeet, other tribes that we didn't know about, who were out west. They were quite different from us,"* she tells me.

Cousin Angel

My cousin Angel is staying with my grandma.

Angel had the opportunity to travel to Ireland and Paris to see the Eiffel Tower, amongst other places in Europe. Grandma tells me, *"I wish I had a chance to do something like that when I was young."* She lives vicariously through Angel's experiences.

Cornelius

It is my nephew Archer's Birthday, my grandma's first great grandchild. My grandma was in tears as she described how Archer's middle name, Cornelius, was my grandma's maiden name. It is beautiful to see her overflowing love for Archer.

She is like a stream of love, flowing through different generations. I can feel the generational love flow through me, too.

Ohana

Sometimes I struggle with not feeling Native enough within the Native American community. I can be questioned due to my light skin and sea blue eyes. When I am with my Ohana, my friends, I feel seen as a human being regardless of my physical attributes. Thanks for loving me as I am and for who I am: John D., John G., John J., Sean, James K., James W., Ryan, Calvin, Bill, Ian, Brent, Darren, Max, Hayden, Eric C., Miller E, and Zach. For all those I did not name, I love you.

II. Acknowledge, Educate, and Honor

Traditional Names

It is possible for Oneida people to be granted a traditional name. My grandmother, mother, sisters, and I all have traditional Oneida names.

"Grandma, do you remember how the traditional naming ceremony goes for Oneida people?"

"I went to the house of an elder, one of the matriarchs of the tribe to give me a name. I sat and talked with her, and she said your name is, 'She has Good Words.'"

"I love that so much. 'She has Good words.' And mine is 'He is a Good Man.'"

"And you have lived up to your name."

"I try to, Granny Bird. You saying that means the world to me. I try to be a better man today than I was yesterday, every day."

"Oh, honey. Well, you truly have."

"You have been so instrumental in my life. I can't thank you enough, Granny Bird. You have always had good words. Even in your prayers, I can feel your good words."

When I was 9 years old, my grandma returned to the elder's home to bestow my traditional name. The elder asked my grandma thoughtful questions about me for 10 minutes or so. She concluded, "He is a Good Boy" and then corrected herself, "Let's call him 'He is a Good Man' so he will grow into a good man."

Pow Wow

I was 19 when I went to my first Pow Wow in Oneida, Wisconsin with my grandma, mom, and sisters, Chelsea and Katelyn.

My sister Chelsea recalls, "Even though we didn't go to Oneida with Grandma until we were older, she took us to several Pow Wows with mom growing up and I remember eating fry bread (with butter and cinnamon) for the first time when I was around my daughter, Hazel's age (age 7). TJ, you were little, but you were there!"

This was the first time I had learned I went to Pow Wows in the Pacific Northwest growing up. I was apparently 3 years old when I went to my first Pow Wow ever.

My grandma recounts, *"When I found out there were Pow Wows in Seattle, I took the kids. I remember carrying my granddaughter, Chelsea, and one of the men in regalia walked by. His feathers brushed her face and she smiled."*

"I didn't wear regalia when I just wanted to watch and check out the stands for handmade beaded crafts, but when I went with my friends, I would wear my regalia and dance."

The Oneida Pow Wow happens annually on the 4th of July weekend. Tribal members travel near and far to sing, dance, celebrate, and eat fry bread.

Community Peacemaking

My grandma scanned pages of our past in her living room, while I learned in the present moment, attending an International Restorative Justice workshop via my iron horse, my laptop. My grandma and my cousin Edi Cornelius-Gropkf taught me graciously with wisdom and humility an indigenous, Haudenosaunee-specific approach to talking circles, called community peacemaking and restorative justice. I disclose to my grandma I felt like an impostor at times teaching about the origins of restorative justice and how it is used in various Indigenous communities, while learning my own traditional practices myself.

She responds compassionately saying, *"We are all learning."*

I love my grandma. Her words water my soul.

Later, I presented my Oneida co-collaborators' and my findings on the sacred game of lacrosse to the Oneida Business Committee, which received a unanimous vote for support. I log on to work for the National Training Center for Restorative Justice at the University of San Diego. Everything I do is to honor my ancestors and pave the way for seven generations to come.

Value

"My parents really didn't know how important an education was," my grandma voiced. *"Things have changed a lot."*

She spoke to me about the perception of Native Americans.

"Oftentimes, Native Americans were perceived from non-Native people as uneducated and savages."

Oneida Hymn Singers

My grandma tells me about the Oneida hymn singers. She said, *"They would sing through the whole night"* at funerals. She describes there would be people outflowing into different rooms. My grandma said, *"They believed someone needed to be around the body. Around midnight or so they would take a break for sandwiches, cake, and coffee, then they would sing again until morning."*

The Kahliwisaks (Our Oneida Nation newspaper, which translates to, "She Looks for News") taught me the Oneida Singers predate Christianity and colonization, as was Oneida tradition to have singers present with the body.

My grandma told me she has been singing a lot lately and they sang this past Sunday afternoon. *"You already had that picture of us,"* from a post I sent her on Facebook messenger of the Oneida Hymn singers at an event.

My grandma shared with me the Oneida Hymn singers have a big event on the 31st. She says, *"It is for a health issue. The Oneida Hymn Singers are getting paid to do it."*

I told her that makes her a professional singer.

She laughed. *"No,"* she said. *"We just like to sing."*

My grandma shared, *"I have to call our cousin Emilie, to learn from our other cousin Edna about the little talk Edna did between each Oneida Hymn song at our last event. Edna talked about where the songs came from. Edna says the songs came from New York. Edna was teaching how the Oneidas would sit under a tree and listen during these other people's meetings. The Oneidas in New York loved the songs. Edna says, they put their own song to the harmony. So, it is a practice which was brought from New York to Wisconsin."*

My grandma continued, *"I used to listen to the Oneida songs on the way to work and the way home from work on a tape. I enjoyed it. I should have kept up with it though. Carol was the leader of the Oneida Hymn Singers for a long time. Carol died, and her daughter remains. Carol's daughter wants to put the Oneida Hymn songs on an app."*

My grandma expressed, *"I don't want the songs and language lost. So many of the old-time singers are dying. The Oneida Hymn Singers are passionate about keeping songs alive."*

A couple other singers, including Rose and Shirley, my grandma's cousin, also died recently. These were all people that sang.

I offered my idea to Granny that they should put their Oneida Hymn singing on YouTube.

Family Gathering

My grandma invited some relatives over for a talking circle. My cousin, Edi Cournelius-Groskopf, led the talking circle, and modeled it for me to learn from. My Great Uncle Leonard, my cousin Norma, my cousin Emily, my Great Aunt Josie, and My great Onkel (uncle in German) Tom joined us.

It was special.
My family showed up for me, for the talking circle, and for singing Oneida Hymns.

The whole time my heart was bursting from the seams to say thank you, but when I tried to speak, the words could not come out. Saying thank you did not do justice to how I felt.

Thank you did not feel sufficient to capture the deep gratitude for my families' love.

Christianity and Colonization

Christianity and colonization often go hand in hand, and complicates my identity, family identity, and spirituality.

At my grandma's Christian church in Oneida, instead of a cross as a symbol, there is a turtle, representing Turtle Island, or North America, with a great White Fur Tree of Peace growing off its back, with two crosses on the tree trunk. One cross is to recognize the atonement of Jesus' sacrifice, and another cross is to recognize the atonement of Indigenous peoples who gave their life for us to live in the way we do now.

The Papal Bull by the Pope in 1493, known as the Doctrine of Discovery, used the term "Terra Nullius" deeming lands not inhabited by Christian peoples to be empty Earth. This Papal Bull was cited as legal grounds for a court case against the Oneida Nation of New York in the 1990's.

Columbus' voyages led to the Doctrine of Discovery. He enslaved over 5,000 Indigenous Peoples. Columbus wrote in his diaries:

> "They do not bear arms, and do not know them, for I showed them a sword, they took it by the edge and cut themselves out of ignorance. They have no iron. Their spears are made of cane... They would make fine servants... With fifty men we could subjugate them all and make them do whatever we want... As soon as I arrived in the Indies, on the first Island which I found. I took some of the natives by force in order that they might learn and might give me information of whatever there is in these parts."

Under Columbus' rule, it is documented that when mining quotas were not met by the Native peoples, their hands were cut off and they bled to death.

A meme circulated using an image from the TV show, *Columbo* with the text, "By the way, when you so called 'discovered America,' was there anyone else there at the time?" A shirt we wore with the American Indian Student Organization at the University of San Diego on Kumeyaay Territory presented a counter-narrative, "Native Americans discovered Columbus lost at sea."

At Pepperdine University, my undergraduate, there was a Christopher Columbus statue. My Grandma saw the statue when she dropped me off at college and was horrified. She took a picture in front of the statue holding her thumbs down with an upset face. The statue was en route to various classes, including my Humanities class, over my 4 and a half years at Pepperdine.

The Columbus statue was not relocated during my time as a student there between 2008 and 2012. I begged the administration to remove the statue. I even lobbied for a debate highlighting both sides of the issue concerning the Columbus statue. I was pushed aside and ridiculed by faculty, administrators, and students for my desire to debate and remove the Columbus statue at Pepperdine.

In 2020, when many statues were being removed by force, the Pepperdine administration preemptively relocated the Columbus statue to Pepperdine University's Florence, Italy Campus.

The piercing gaze and point of the statue remains etched in my mind to this day knowing how his existence changed the fate for the Indigenous population on turtle island.

Constitution

Back in Elementary school, my grandmother would tell me, *"You know, the Iroquois influenced our Constitution in the United States,"* to which I would stubbornly say, "Grandma, if that was true, I would have learned that in school."

But it was true.

The Iroquois, known in our own language as the Haudenosaunee, meaning the People of the Longhouse, did influence our system of governance in the United States and I did not learn it in school.

My grandma told me, *"The people coming in [settlers] considered them [Native Americans] ignorant savages. Many of the U.S. leaders back then, when talking about forming the United States, would say 'this is what we did, we did this.' So no one knew it [where it had come from]. And if the U.S. leaders did know it, they would take credit for it."*

The State of New York's public school curriculum teaches that the Haudenosaunee, the Iroquois word for Iroquois, did in fact influence the United States Constitution, the system of federalism, and checks and balances. House Concurrent Resolution 331 from 1988 documents the Haudenosaunee influence on the founding of our country, put forth by our 100th Congress of the United States. Scholars like Ronald Grinde, Barbara Alice Mann, Jerry Fields, Bruce Johansen, Richard W. Hill Sr., and Oren Lyons, among others, have written and spoken about the Haudenosaunee influence on the formation of the United States.

Many of the Haudenosaunee and US ideals overlap, as the formation of the United States was directly inspired and influenced by the Haudenosaunee form of government. The analogy I share with people is that the Haudenosaunee is like the book, and the United States is the movie based on the book. Did the movie miss some key elements of the book? Such as consensus decision making for the Haudenosaunee and two-thirds majority population voting for the United States? Or how the Haudenosaunee had clan mothers since 1142 in a role equivalent to the Supreme Court, whereas the United States allowed women to vote in only 1920? Indeed, some key differences. However, can films be remade? Absolutely. They can be updated, retconned, and reimagined. A remake of a film can tell the same story, yet be like a whole new movie. The United States is due for a film remake, more closely aligned with the inspired manuscript of the Haudenosaunee where we care about those around us, where we recognize we are all connected, where we are reminded we are all still one nation.

The Other Side

Granny has a plot of land for me in Oneida, Wisconsin, next to her parents and some of her siblings.

Why do I want a tombstone out in Oneida, Wisconsin?

I want people to come visit here.
I want people to come see Indigenous people are continuing to carry out their culture despite genocide.

We are peaceful people. We are loving people. We love family. We love friends. We love the Packers. We love traditions. We love language. We love learning. We are modern. We are building. We are creating. We are here. We are imperfect. We love this country. We love our Creator. We are human, just like the rest of us.

Hierarchy

I share with my Indigenous Studies students that the settler colonialism perspective on hierarchy is having human beings dominate on top, animals below us, plants after that, and then Earth on the bottom.

Elders from various Tribal Nations share their perspectives of an inverted world view from the colonists.

For an Indigenous world view, Mother Earth is on top, the plants of all the medicines of the Earth second, followed by the 4-legged and the 2-legged animals, and last and intentionally least, the human-beings, whose jobs are to be stewards of *all* living things above us.

Certainly, a different perspective.

At what point is life not seen as sacred?
We need to recognize the sacred nature of every living thing in the Universe.

I Understand

I practice Community Peacemaking which falls in alignment with Restorative practices. This can be an alternative to mediation but biased for peace and harmony.

The word for understanding in American Sign Language involves gestures around the head, like a lightbulb turning on multiple times. This western perspective demonstrates a logical understanding.

For American Indian Plains Sign Language, it involves gestures around the heart. This encompasses a logical understanding, but further extends to a connection between hearts.

The beautiful storytelling of the word "understand" in the different sign languages reflect a deeper philosophy for the different cultures.

I appreciate this sentiment of understanding involving both our head and our heart. Don Coyhis states the 18-inches traveled from someone's head to their heart is the longest journey a human being will travel in their lifetime.

Assassin's Creed 3

Grandma
This video game I got
you play as a Mohawk person
Mohawk characters speak in their native language
with English subtitles
It is so cool and powerful to hear it spoken!
Some similarities to Oneida from my barely trained ear

"You're right," she tells me.
"It does sound similar to Oneida.
When I was living in Seattle,
my friend Jeanne's mother invited us to her church because there were going to be Seneca missionaries speaking.
We went and when they sang,
It was the same as ours.
I recognized the song
and it was our same language."

Thanksgiving & Native American Heritage Day

I was in Oneida for Thanksgiving in 2022 and this holiday was referred to as Native American Heritage Day. I am grateful for the acknowledgement, education, and honor of my ancestors.

In 1637, Governor John Winthrop of the Massachusetts Bay Colony proclaimed on Thanksgiving Day, "A day of thanksgiving kept in all the churches for our victories against the Pequots…" He is referencing a massacre by colonists from the Massachusetts Bay Colony of burning down a village of anywhere from 300 to 800 Pequot Native peoples in their sleep. The colonists then thanked God for this action.

Thanksgiving, according to, Brittanica.com is described as:
"Colonists in New England and Canada regularly observed 'thanksgivings,' of prayer for such blessings as safe journeys, military victories, or abundant harvests."

These military victories were often massacres of Native peoples.

My mind cannot escape the heaviness from the past when I see the references of happy depictions of Pilgrims with Indians. This conceals the truth of extermination and genocide done to Native peoples as a result of colonization. I cannot unlearn these stories I have learned and Thanksgiving has since been a heavy day of mourning for me in knowing the truth about the massacres occurring against tribes over Thanksgiving past. I usually cry uncontrollably in a closet before attempting to calm myself and share a meal with loved ones.

However, this past trip changed everything. Experiencing Native American Heritage Day with my grandmother and extended family on the reservation in Oneida, Wisconsin was profoundly healing for myself.

I will never think of this day of Thanksgiving and Native American Heritage Day the same again. Yes, it is Thanksgiving and Native American Heritage Day. It is yes and, not either or.

We have reclaimed the holiday to be a joyful day of appreciation, beauty, and family. I am healing. Healing is a process, not an event. When we heal ourselves, we heal our ancestors.

Santa's Real

My grandma recalled, *"When I was young, we would go to sleep on Christmas Eve and there would be nothing set up. When us kids were sleeping, my dad would go into the forest behind the house and find a big tree. He would bring it in the house, decorate the tree, and set up all the gifts. When we woke up, there would be all these gifts I knew my parents could not afford. That is how I knew Santa was real when I was a little girl."*

Hoyá·n! Happy New Year

Hoyá·n means "Happy New Year" in Oneida.

My grandma shared, *"When I was young, we would go door-to-door to neighbor's houses on New Year's with a paper bag. We would stand outside the door and say, 'Hoyá·n' and neighbors would fill our paper bags with donuts."*

This tradition is said to have originated around the 1600's in the cultural interactions between the Haudenosaunee and the Dutch as they formed a treaty. It is Dutch tradition to ring in the New Year with a celebration of donuts.

The Hoyá·n Haudenosaunee practice is also recognized by the Onondaga, Oneidas, Tuscarora, and Six Nations of the Grand River in Canada. This tradition is continued by some to this day, including celebrations in Oneida, Wisconsin. Some people still make their own doughnuts, while others buy them pre-made from stores.

My family celebrates Hoyá·n with homemade or store-bought donuts. It warms my grandma's heart and is a family tradition we look forward to sharing together.

Reservation Dogs

My grandma and I binge watched *Reservation Dogs* when I visited her this past summer. We were joking today about how her dog, Elvis, is a reservation dog.

Reservation Dogs is a culturally relevant show in how it showcases Native communities.

We finished watching an episode titled, "Come and Get Your Love." It talks about a myth of a Deer Woman, who has hooves like a deer and lures bad men in with her looks to kill them.

After we finish the episode, my grandma goes, *"Oh. Oh."*

My Grandma generally does not just say, "Oh, oh" unless she is offended, hurt, or surprised.

I say, "Grandma, what's wrong?"

She replies, *"There is a story about a Deer Man in Oneida."*

"Some time ago in Oneida there was a big gathering where everyone was dancing. There was this very handsome man that was walking around, and he got all the women's attention, even the married ones. Then, all of a sudden, they all see the man has hooves. Right then, the man jumped over them onto a roof and ran away on his hooves."

The tone shifted and I got the chills.

Civilization

My grandma speaks about Tom Porter, who shares Iroquois knowledge in his book, "And Grandma Said... Iroquois Teachings."

"It's good it's taught in New York," she tells me.
"It should be taught all over, Nationwide. The founding fathers, they don't want to give too much credit. They believed they were savages, uncivilized."

I shared with my grandma about a Trudell civilization quote, "The great lie is that it is civilization. It's not civilized. It has literally been the most blood thirsty brutalizing system ever imposed on this planet. That is not civilization. That's the great lie- is that it represents civilization. That's the great lie. Or if it does represent civilization and that's truly what civilization is, then the great lie is that civilization is good for us."

She nods slowly with eyebrows raised.

Drum

During the Oneida Pow Wow, I do a traditional dance called Smoke Dance. The winner gets a prize.

My grandma does not know for certain whether my families' ancestors smoked danced or not. Granny and my cousin Norma Skenandore Primeau dance in the genre of traditional women's.

Up until the American Indian Religious Freedom Act of 1978, Native peoples were forbidden from practicing their traditional ceremonies and practicing their traditional beliefs.

The first Oneida Pow Wow in Wisconsin was in 1972. Often regalia was worn that showcased stars and stripes, so people dancing could hide their culture in plain sight while meeting the approval of Bureau of Indian Affairs agents who thought the people dancing were merely showcasing their love for the United States. The Oneida in Wisconsin do have a deep love and appreciation for the United States, and for our own sovereign culture as Oneida people, which predates colonization.

You dance wearing full regalia. The regalia is clothing which allows a person to express themselves, with cultural and spiritual significance. For each genre of Native dancing, there is a style of regalia to be worn.

When dancing, it is a race between the drummers pounding the drum and singing, and the dancers trying to keep pace with the drumbeat. People dance as swift as possible with style and unique expression in a fast-paced freestyle dance, dancing to the beat of the speedy-paced drum.

The idea for dancing in traditional Native dances is to hear the drum beat like your mother's heartbeat, when you were in the womb. Dancing is to take you back to that place in time, when you were one with your mother's heartbeat.

Intergenerational Trauma and Intergenerational Resiliency

Recently, I was working through intergenerational trauma with my therapist. She spoke about when it is important to witness historical trauma versus when it is appropriate to put up boundaries to recognize what is mine to process. Native American historical and intergenerational trauma is good to process and work through, however, there is a difference of what mine is to carry, what mine is to process, and how I can best support relatives through witnessing and holding space.

By holding space for a relative experiencing intergenerational trauma, we are utilizing intergenerational strength to support one another. My therapist reminded me if we want to truly show up and help someone we love, we need to be in a place of strength to have the ability to hold space and support our loved one.

Part of breaking the cycle of intergenerational trauma is recognizing boundaries of what is acceptable. My therapist, a person of Judaic heritage, reminded me to put up boundaries to say that trauma is unacceptable.

In an article by the Huffington Post on July 1, 2022, the author, Se-ah-dom Edmo, stated the design of colonization is to "keep us poor, keep us ignorant, keep us divided, and keep us sick." I find we can combat this with contrasting logic, such as by thriving financially, educating ourselves as Native peoples, unifying in solidarity, and healing ourselves and our world.

I really do think we can change this world. I no longer accept the trauma that runs through my veins and tries to define me. I meet trauma with success, strength, and resiliency.

If anyone showed me these things, my grandma did. My grandma worked a forklift in the back warehouse of JC Penny until retirement. She has always been a consistent financial pillar for me. If not for the support of her, my family, and my wife, I do not think I would be alive today.

I remember times in my life where I would have to skip meals for a day or so at a time because I did not have money. I remember driving to work, running on fumes about to run out of gas. I would call my grandma in a sweet voice and say, "Grandma, do you think you could by chance send me some money so I could get gas to go to work?" And my grandma's response was always, "*Of course, sweetheart. Why didn't you tell me sooner?*" My grandma never scolded me, berated me, lectured me, or looked down upon me when I had no money to my name, just debt. My grandma was able to thrive financially to help me up the ladder to do the same.

Garden

I asked my grandma where she feels most at home, having the most fun, feeling most filled with life. She responded, *"my garden."*

Granny will spend hours in her garden. Even when her body is sore and weak, her spirit is in the garden.

She has about 50 plants out in her yard. All the seeds fall into the ground and sprout up again.

During my visits, I would spend time with her outside in the garden. My grandma would be out working in the garden for hours. I would be in decent shape from training for lacrosse, yet every time I would be ready to go inside long before my grandma would.

My grandma would ask, *"Could you wheel that stool over here, please?"* She would proceed to pull weeds and tend to her vegetables.

"I have an infestation of tomatoes and cucumbers in my garden."
I tell her she has been blessed.

She responds, *"I am going to take a bunch of tomatoes and cucumbers to the church to give out to others."*

When our Great Creator blesses her, she blesses others.

Traditionally as Haudenosaunee people, we plant the three sisters: corn, beans, and squash as they grow in harmony with one another. The corn grows tall, the beans wrap around the corn stalk, and the squash creates natural shade for the base of the corn and beans to help them have an ideal ecological niche. The three sisters' vegetables grown together provide long term soil fertility.

When colonists first arrived on the shores, they scoffed and ridiculed the Native peoples, thinking Native peoples had inferior agricultural methods because Europe used monocropping. Recent scientific studies through a western lens have supported the rich benefit of having corn, beans, and squash grown together. My scientist sister, Chelsea, explains squash prevents soil erosion and beans fix nitrogen in the soil that other plants benefit from.

Homecoming

The Oneida Hymn singers had a meeting at grandma's house.

They recently sang for the children that died decades ago at Carlisle Indian Boarding School and were returned to the Oneida reservation to be repatriated.

When we die, we will eventually decompose to the Earth and return back to the soil. According to the National Institute of Health, "human mitochondrial DNA can persist in grave soil and be consistently detected throughout decomposition."

These children had a homecoming to their homelands. They were given the proper burial and honor they deserved after all this time. Their families were able to grieve them in their eternal resting home on the soil of their ancestors.

My grandma said it was two children who were repatriated and honored this time, and it will be three children to be repatriated the next.

Singers would sing all night in the olden days when someone passed.
This time they sang for five minutes.

In Canada, these schools were called, "Indian Residential Schools." In the United States, these institutions were called, "Indian Boarding Schools." The Kentucky Government website stated the Choctaw Indian Academy opened in 1825. According to the National Centre for Truth and Reconciliation in Canada, the first Indian Residential School was opened in 1831. Carlisle Indian Boarding School was opened in 1879, where the motto of the school was to, "kill the Indian to save the man." Carlisle Indian Boarding School was one of the most well-known Indian Boarding Schools and would be used as an archetype for over 450 Indian Boarding Schools in the United States. There were over 150 Indian Residential Schools in Canada.

There is discrepancy over exactly how many Indian Boarding and Residential School children were killed at these institutions. In May 2021, the Kamloops Indian Residential School unearthed 215 First Nations children who were killed and never able to return home. Carlisle Indian School was found to have 180 tombstones for children killed, and another 13 tombstones for children who were unidentifiable when they were killed.

According to the On Canada Project, as of March 2022, there have been 10,028 children's bodies discovered. This is after investigating a handful of the 150 Indian Residential Schools, and one of the over 450 Indian Boarding Schools, Carlisle Indian Boarding School, in the United States.

According to the United Nations Article II Convention on the Prevention and Punishment of the Crime of Genocide, "Genocide means any of the following acts committed with intent to destroy, in whole or in part, a national, ethnical, racial or religious group, as such:
1. Killing members of the group;
2. Causing serious bodily or mental harm to members of the group;

3. Deliberately inflicting on the group conditions of life calculated to bring about its physical destruction in whole or in part;
4. Imposing measures intended to prevent births within the group;
5. Forcibly transferring children of the group to another group."

Here is a breakdown, point-by-point, throughout history.

"Killing members of the group": This would include all the Indian Residential and Boarding School children who were killed, including my great, great Uncle Joshua. Conservatively, this number is in the tens of thousands, likely substantially in the hundreds of thousands. My great grandpa, Anderson, talked about hearing the cries of babies who were being burnt alive, after a Native girl would give birth to a child after being sexually assaulted by a priest or school worker. My great grandpa talked about smelling the babies' flesh being burned and seeing the babies' bones in the furnace after. This is the definition of infanticide.

More than 53 different forced marches occurred against Native peoples in the United States, the more well-known being the Trail of Tears.

The California missions were built by enslaved Indigenous peoples and each Mission is a mass burial site of Indigenous enslaved people who were killed in creating the Missions. Bounties were paid to California settlers in the state's early years, paying $.25 in 1856 and $5 in 1860 for the scalp or head of a Native person. This policy lasted until 1903 in California.

On August 21, 2021, the Governor of Colorado rescinded an 1864 order to kill Native Americans.

In *The Indian as Peacemaker* by Mary Powers (1932), she eloquently articulated,

> It was only as the white man encroached more and more, as he drove the Indian farther and farther toward the setting sun, that the red man did retaliate and take a stand for national existence. Every white man who fought for home, country, or religion is considered a patriot; but every Indian who did likewise is termed a murderous savage (Powers, 1932, p. 11).

"Causing serious bodily or mental harm to members of the group": It is estimated that sexual abuse occurred between 90 to 100% of students who attended the Indian Boarding and Residential Schools. Indian Boarding and Residential School survivors talk about school officials showing students how to wash themselves in the shower, every day, through their teenage years. At the Indian Boarding Schools, Native American students were forbidden to speak their Tribal languages and were beaten, had their mouths washed out, or killed. Students who spoke the same language were often placed at different schools, and siblings were separated and forbidden to speak their Native language with each other. Native American students' hair was cut when the students first arrived. This traditionally would occur if a male had someone close to him pass away. It is estimated that over 90% of Native children were stripped from their homes. If parents resisted, they were arrested. People who were descendants of someone who went through the Indian Boarding or Residential Schools are considered survivors. It was often not the person who survived through the Indian Boarding and Residential Schools themselves who committed suicide, more often it was the descendants of those students who committed suicide in this chain of intergenerational trauma.

"Deliberately inflicting on the group conditions of life calculated to bring about its physical destruction in whole or in part": This can be seen through federal policy towards Native peoples. This would include the still active Doctrine of Discovery, which was created in 1493, stating any lands not inhabited by Christian peoples would be considered Terra Nulius, or vacant land. The Indian Removal Act of 1830 legalized federal extermination of Native peoples through forced removal from peoples' traditional lands and food sources. In the land of freedom of religion, it would not be until 1978 that the American Indian Religious Freedom Act was passed. In 1990, the Native American Languages Act would legalize the speaking of Native American languages, even though 33 different Tribal Nations used their Native languages as code talkers to aid the US military. The more well-known Code Talkers would be the Diné, also known as Navajo. In 1968, the military declassified this information.

In Article 1, Section 8, Clause 3 of the Constitution, otherwise known as the Indian Commerce Clause, the United States federal government outlines how it is to interact with Tribal Nations, in the same way they do with different states and international governments. The Supremacy Clause of the Constitution, Article VI, paragraph 2, states all Treaties with Tribal Nations are the supreme law of the land. You can go on digitreaties.org and look at the 374 ratified treaties, which had over two-thirds approval by the House of Representatives and the Senate and were signed by the President of the United States. It is known many of these treaties were made under false pretense, had an unauthorized Tribal member sign the form, or used coercion, lies, or alcohol to induce people into an agreeable state. In 1908, the Supreme Court Case of Lonewolf v. Hithcock stated the United States Congress has the right to modify or terminate treaties with Tribal Nations without the Native peoples' consent.

"Imposing measures intended to prevent births within the group": In the 1970's, it is estimated doctors in the United States sterilized 25 to 42% of Native women who were near childbearing age, some who were as young as 15 years old.

"Forcibly transferring children of the group to another group": The Sixties Scoop occurred in Canada in the 1960's when policies allowed First Nations children to be scooped up by Canadian government workers and placed in foster homes without consent, also known as kidnapping. The Indian Child Welfare Act of 1978, or ICWA, "recognize[s] the essential tribal relations of Indian people and the cultural and social standards prevailing in Indian communities and families." ICWA was being heard before the US Constitution in November 2022, to decide whether ICWA is constitutional under the Equal Protection Clause. If ICWA is found unconstitutional it will undermine Federal Indian Law and Tribal Nations as sovereigns.

This is just the tip of the iceberg. I feel sick to my stomach engaging with the heaviness of it all. It is honestly hard to talk about. Thinking of what really happened at those schools and how little the general public knows about it, is tough and sickening as a third-generation survivor of the Indian Boarding Schools. I had one of my students at the law school I teach at encourage me that if I do not tell the full details of what happened, then I am doing injustice to the people who had to endure those things.

When you help heal yourself, you help heal the world. When you heal, you can help your ancestors heal, whose blood runs through you, who never had a chance to heal.

Pendleton

My grandma told me, "*I went to the Pow Wow in Keshena. I got Pendleton luggage.*"
She was so excited.
My grandma has everything Pendleton in her house.

Pendleton blankets are given away at Pow Wows or gifted by elders as a way to honor people. There is a rising conversation, particularly from the younger generation of Natives, on the ethics of supporting Native brands created by Native artists versus Native inspired brands, which are brands inspired by Native culture without Native artists.

Pendleton is not owned by Native American people, which would fall under the Native inspired category.

The Pendleton Company states on their website, under history, and the timeline date of 1909:

"The production of blankets resumed as the Bishops applied intuitive business concepts for quality products and distinctive styling. A study of the color and design preferences of local and Southwest Native Americans resulted in vivid colors and intricate patterns. Trade expanded from the Nez Perce nation near Pendleton to the Navajo, Hopi and Zuni nations. These Pendleton blankets were used as basic wearing apparel and as a standard of value for trading and credit among Native Americans. The blankets also became prized for ceremonial use."

In contrast, Eighth Generation is an "Inspired Native" Brand. They showcase this stance on their website:
"'Inspired Natives®, not "Native-inspired.' Eighth Generation is a Seattle based art and lifestyle brand owned by the Snoqualmie Tribe. We partner with community-based Native artists around the country to design, manufacture and market beautiful wool blankets and gifts intended for everyone around the globe. In doing so, we are boldly reclaiming control over the market for products featuring Native art and the stories that go with them – all while building the business capacity of our artist partners through the Inspired Natives® Project."

I love my grandma's Pendleton luggage, towels, and blankets.
I am inspired by Eighth Generation.

I want to be part of the future. I am motivated to create my own clothing company, called "1142," referencing the year the Haudenosaunee came together under the Great Law of Peace, which the US Constitution was based on.

III. Good Man and Good Words

License

"*I like how you express yourself in writing,*" my grandma tells me.
All those years of schooling must have paid off.

In the movie, *Good Will Hunting*, there is a scene where Skylar says how much her brain is worth. I do some rough calculations in an excel sheet and find out the appraisal worth is currently: $503,015. I tell my grandma and without skipping a beat she says, *"I know it is worth more than that."*

During my PhD, it was about knowing the rules of academic writing. Now as a writer, it is knowing when to break those rules and defy the confines of strict academic writing.

I am at liberty to use my poetic license.

I remember learning about a poetic license when I was a freshman in high school. I decided I wanted one of those someday. I silently thought to myself I would need to find out how to acquire one of these cards and where I needed to go to apply.

Truth

Maybe we will all wake up someday
Look around
And want to seek the truth
Want to learn our past
Where do we come from?
Who lived here for thousands of years?

Keys

My grandma makes life vibrant. Currently, she is practicing locking herself out of the house to see if her keys work.

Remembering

It is the anniversary of September 11th. My heart shatters remembering the tragedy and goes out to all those impacted.

As a 6th grader in California, I watched the news with my mom in silence with her hand over her mouth, listened on the radio on the way to school in our neighborhood carpool in silence, and then watched it at home period.

My grandma says, *"I remember where I was. I was visiting Oneida, Wisconsin, where I live now, from the Pacific Northwest. I was out to eat with some relatives, and we watched the plane hit the building, thinking it was an accident. As the news unfolded, I found out all flights were grounded."*

ABC 20/20 is doing a feature about different babies whose fathers died as firefighters on 9/11.

One of the people in the ABC special, "The Babies of 9/11, 20 Years Later" talked about how he wanted to become a doctor, because during the pandemic, he saw people run away from the public health crisis and saw people that stepped toward it wanting to help. He wanted to be one of those people.

He has a pure heart to emulate the service of his father.

This is similar to the calling I feel for public service.
Out of love for this country, I plan to try to make it better for all people.

Drawing the Circle Bigger

I fear we as human beings still have a capacity for ugliness, cruelty, prejudice, and evil.

My grandma has one of the best hearts in the world, and tells me *how much she loves my wife*, who is half-Mexican and half-Syrian, two groups of many that have been the target of discrimination.

My heart breaks when I see and hear people experience prejudice.

All people are inhabitants across this Mother Earth. We all breathe the same air. In the words of Dr. Donald Warne, "Let us remember, we all drink from the same stream of consciousness. We are all connected by that same stream of consciousness. We are all related. What we do to each other, we do to ourselves. Act kindly toward my people, for indeed my people are your people."

Edwin Markham (1852-1940) wrote,

"He drew a circle that shut me out-
Heretic, rebel, a thing to flout.
But love and I had the wit to win:
We drew a circle and took him In!"
This poem strikes me every time I recall it.
I am constantly learning to make the circle of inclusion bigger.

My sister, Chelsea, once told my dad, "What is so bad about wanting to be mindful of others with our words? What is wrong with being inclusive?"

I love these questions and ask others to ask themselves the same.

We are created to love our Creator and love others.
When we love ourselves, we love the world.

First Dream

My first dream was to be an astronaut. After an optometrist visit in second grade, I found out I was color impaired, shattering my ability to join the Air Force. I had only watched the NASA Training Camp VHS about 100 times. My 7-year-old heart was devastated.

After that, and through high school, I wanted to be a firefighter. I held onto this dream until it dawned on me, I was not physically gifted enough to be a firefighter.

When I was a freshman in college, my public speaking instructor, Greg Daum, played a video of Robert Kennedy giving an impromptu eulogy for Dr. King in Indianapolis, Indiana on April 4, 1968. Prior to this, people had convinced me all politicians were evil. Seeing Bobby Kennedy use his oratory and leadership skills to unite people in the wake of a tragedy, I knew I wanted to be a public servant to use my gifts for good. The thread of wanting to help people continues to propel me toward my calling.

5/25/21

"TJ
You are brilliant.
Write that down so you don't forget."
- A note from grandma

Love Cups

On the phone with my grandmother, we talked about filling up our own love cups so we can pour into others. I love that imagery. "*I do, too,*" my grandma tells me.

Great Grandkids

"TJ, is your grandma awake? Maybe we can call her?" my wife asks.

I look at the time and respond, "She's probably awake, half-awake half-asleep. Using her iPad to scroll on Facebook, scouring the site for pictures of her great grandkids."

When we tell this to Granny on our next phone call, she laughs and says, *"There's never enough photos."*
We smile.

One of the sweetest and most powerful things is watching the generations connect. Great Grandma Eleanor Bailey, or GG, as she is lovingly called by the little ones, is deeply connected to her great grandchildren, my sister Chelsea's three children, Archer Cornelius Sterrett, Hazel Katerina Sterrett, and Penelope Rey Sterrett. They love their great grandma and great grandma loves them with all her heart. This special bond connects the 4 generations together. Watching their love pour out for each other, as grandma teaches them stories and songs, is good medicine for my soul and spirit.

Grace

My grandma tells me a story about when she was traveling in her car, *"When I was young, I was at my doctor's office. I was about to pull out, but I paused because it sounded like there was something underneath the car, as if there was metal dragging on the cement.*

I stopped to check, and in that moment a car came by and would have side swiped me had I pulled out further earlier. When I checked there was nothing wrong with the car.

It would have been the end if God didn't stop me.

It was God stepping in to take care of me before I asked or knew. People say it is coincidence or luck. I don't believe in that at all. There are quite a few times where God has protected me. His grace."

Smile

I am about to go teach a class.

My grandma expresses, *"If you see someone without a smile, then give them one of yours."*

This is from my grandma's mom, my Great Grandma Lilliane Rose Cornelius, maiden name Wheelock.

Everything

My grandma tells me,

"You can do everything I wish I had done."

Proud

Granny shares with me, *"I am proud of you. Because of the man you are. Upstanding. Honest. I am proud of you."*

I intend to live up to the meaning of my Oneida name, "He is a Good Man."

Time

My grandma tells me she is 83, but she does not feel 83. She said she still feels 57.
This makes my soul smile.

I ponder all the questions I want to ask my grandma next time I see her. Our time together is so precious. I want to know as much as I can.

A time she remembers laughing the hardest?
The time she danced the hardest?
What is her advice for people going through a hard time?
What is her advice for people going through a good time?
What is one thing you wish you knew growing up?
What should we tell other people?
What do we tell people in our book?
What is a question she has for me?
What does she think I should tell other people?

I just want her to live forever, yet I know death is what brings meaning to our lives. I am grateful I have this time with her, and next time I see her, I will be savoring every word, every ounce of joy, every smile, every laugh, and every memory. I cannot wait to see my grandma again. She is one of my favorite people in the whole world. My grandma is the person I am most like.

In the film, *Smoke Signals*, the actor playing the character Thomas told the director offscreen he was portraying his grandmother through his performance. I resonate with portraying my grandmother in this life.

I ask my grandma the questions from earlier.
My grandma tells me, *"I want the very best for you and will help in any way I can."*

Happy to Get to Know Anyone

"I am glad you got to go to try out for the Haudenosaunee National team in New York in 2015."

My grandma said, *"I am so glad you are so outgoing, so people can invite you to go have breakfast with them,"* which happened to me in New York after my tryout.

She described, *"It is because of you, because you are so happy to get to know anyone."*

I say I got it from her.

She replied, *"I get it from you."*

I say she is sweet.

She added, *"You are sweet."*

We both laughed.
Laughter is abundant whenever we are together or talking.
Our laughter is medicine.

Technology

I call my grandma on her cell phone. She picks up and tells me,
"I don't understand all these modern conveniences."

I say, "I guess you do."
We both laugh.

Beaded Eagle Feather

I tell Granny I was honored with a beaded eagle feather, made by colleague Dr. Kimberly Robertson who is Muscogee. I was recognized for being named a tenure-track faculty in American Indian Studies at California State University of Long Beach, also known as Cal State Puvungna. She is in tears.

My grandma tells me she is living her dream through me.

Respect and Sharing

I am so impressed with my grandma's ability to listen to other people she disagrees with.

She tells me,
"We are welcome to our own beliefs.
Why should I get upset about it?
They have a right to believe what they do."

Bragging

On the phone, I said to my grandma, "Hi Sweet Pea, how are you?"

"I am wonderful, how are you?" she replied.

"I am doing so, so good."

She said knowingly, *"I know you are. We prayed for you in church today. I was bragging about you in church. There were prayers for any concerns or joys. I told the pastor that you are the joy of my life."*

I reply, "That makes me so happy."

"I told her you were teaching."

"You are sweet."

She echoes, *"You are sweeter."*

She then pulled her car into the VFW, the Veterans of Foreign Wars, building in Oneida to practice their Oneida hymn singing.

My grandma tells me about another time they sang recently as Oneida Hymn Singers.

"We drove up there, to Wapacka. Someplace up north to sing. *I am really glad we did. I am not sure if he was Oneida or not. Him and his wife got a divorce. Their son died and she didn't tell him. He just found out about it later on. He wanted to have his own service. There were 10 of us, 5 in each car. Something like that. We went up there, we drove up there. He was really happy. He was crying. He was glad we came up to sing. We had our own little service for him."*

"That is beautiful, Grandma," I replied to her.

"That is what we did yesterday. because there is always a question when someone asks us to sing at a wake when it is not in our own little territory." My grandma shifted the gears of the conversation, *"So anyways, I am at the VFW. Looks like nobody has mowed their lawn."*

We both laughed really hard.

"Would not be easy to mow with the flag poles," she pointed out, and I confirmed.

"2 more cars pulled in. Norma just got here. She just pulled up. We are just practicing to make sure we are good."

"I love that grandma. You are very good."

Someday

My grandma had a sense of concern in her voice. Her inner thoughts disclosed as she revealed, "*Where are all the young people who would sing Oneida Hymns at my funeral someday?*"

"If you die before me, Grandma, I would be an Oneida Hymn Singer at your funeral."

I grew up singing since I was 19 with the Oneida Hymn Singers.

Usually, I just sit next to one of my Great Uncles who were a bass and sing along with them. With my Great Uncle Ben passing away, I have one less singer to sing next to and learn from.

Never Alone

My grandma recalled a dream to me, *"I dreamt about my mom the other day. I said, 'Hey mom.' Then it felt funny. Then when I woke up, I realized how good it felt to say, 'Hi mom.' I hadn't had a dream about her in years. I was so happy when I woke up. I know she is perfectly happy."*

"I still remember having a dream about her and Harry," my grandma continued. *"We were just driving. Harry was still alive back then when I had the dream, when I lived in Seattle. It was very comforting."*

I told my grandma about when I tried out for the Haudenosaunee Nationals Indoor Lacrosse Team in 2015.

I told her I was not asleep or dreaming, but it was kind of like daydreaming.

I was nervous before the tryouts in 2015 and had been praying a lot. On the way to the tryout in New York, I felt my Great Uncle Harry was sitting shotgun, even though he was still alive in a hospital at the time in Wisconsin, and I felt my late Great Grandfather Anderson Cornelius was sitting in the back right, and my late great uncle Lincoln was sitting in the back left, both of whom have passed on from this life to the Sky World.

My grandma reflects, *"You were amongst all lacrosse players."*

"Yeah," I told her. "It felt like this was nothing new to our family," I responded.

"Who would have thought you would do that. Everybody took you in, invited you to eat with them. That was the coolest ever."

"You believed in me and supported me to go."

And then she encouraged me saying, *"You just have to be yourself. People love you."*

First

My grandmother told me, *"There is so much more to say... I've always wanted to write, but find it difficult to express myself. As always, I'm super proud of you. I always believed that you're more intelligent than you think, and you've proved that you are. Let this be just your first book of many."*

Yawʌ²kó, thank you in Oneida, Grandma.
You are my angel.
I love you and so much of my love as a person comes from you.
Everything I do, I do for you.

Always Remember

This is a truth my grandmother told me,

"Kunolúkhwa means I love you,"

Kunolúkhwa, Dodo. I love you, Grandma.
Always remember.

Nʌkiʔwah, Until Next Time

We are healing. We are whole. We love you, my family and I. You are worthy of love. Each and every one of us. While we cannot change the past, we can learn from it to create a more just, equitable, and loving society for all peoples and for seven generations to come. I have heard it said we repeat what we do not repair. By acknowledging and educating, we are honoring these peoples' stories and transforming trauma into resilience.

Appendix of Photos

Published by Phia Studios © Teelia Pelletier
ISBN: 978-1-953216-00-7

www.ingramcontent.com/pod-product-compliance
Lightning Source LLC
Chambersburg PA
CBHW080456170426
43196CB00016B/2823